OUR OBLIGATION CONCERNING THE COMPANIONS

تأليف
عبد الرزاق بن عبد المحسن البدر
غفر الله له ولوالديه وللمسلمين

SHAYKH ABDUR RAZZĀQ AL-BADR

ISBN: 978-1-9451-7884-9

First Edition: Dhul Qiddah 1437 A.H. / August 2016 C.E.

Cover Design: Pario Studio, UK

Translation by Abū Sulaymān Muḥammad ʿAbdul-ʿAẓīm Ibn Joshua Baker

Revision & Editing by ʿAbdullāh Omrān

Typesetting & formatting by Abū Sulaymān Muḥammad ʿAbdul-ʿAẓīm Ibn Joshua Baker

Printing: Ohio Printing

Subject: ʾUsūl Dīn / Minhāj

Website: www.maktabatulirshad.com
E-mail: info@maktabatulirshad.com

Table of Contents

BRIEF BIOGRAPHY OF THE AUTHOR

His name: Shaykh 'Abdur-Razzāq Ibn 'Abdul-Muhsin al-'Abbād al-Badr.

He is the son of the *'Allāmah* and *Muhaddith* of Madīnah Shaykh 'Abdul-Muhsin al 'Abbād al-Badr.

Birth: He was born on the 22nd day of *Dhul-Qa'dah* in the year 1382 AH in az-Zal'fi, Kingdom of Saudi Arabia. He currently resides in Madīnah.

Current Occupation: He is a member of the teaching staff at the Islāmic University of Madīnah.

Scholarly Certifications: Doctorate in *'Aqīdah.*

The Shaykh has authored books, papers of research, as well as numerous explanations in different disciplines. Among them are:

1. *Fiqh of Supplications & adh-Kār.*
2. *Hajj & Refinement of Souls.*

3. Explanation of '*Exemplary Principles*' by Shaykh Ibn 'Uthaymīn (رَحِمَهُ ٱللَّهُ).

4. Explanation of the book, *The Principles of Names & Attributes*, authored by Shaykh-ul-Islām Ibn al-Qayyim (رَحِمَهُ ٱللَّهُ).

5. Explanation of the book, *Good Words*, authored by Shaykh-ul-Islām Ibn al-Qayyim (رَحِمَهُ ٱللَّهُ).

6. Explanation of the book, al-'Aqīdah *at-Tahāwiyyah.*

7. Explanation of the book, *Fusūl: Biography of the Messenger*, by Ibn Kathīr (رَحِمَهُ ٱللَّهُ).

8. An explanation of the book, *al-Adab-ul-Mufrad*, authored by Imām Bukhārī (رَحِمَهُ ٱللَّهُ).

He studied knowledge under a number of scholars; the most distinguishable of them are:

1. His father the *'Allāmah* Shaykh 'Abdul-Muhsin al-Badr (حفظه الله).

2. The *'Allāmah* Shaykh Ibn Bāz (رَحِمَهُ ٱللَّهُ).

3. The *'Allāmah* Shaykh Muḥammad Ibn Sālih al-'Uthaymīn (رَحِمَهُ ٱللَّهُ).

4. Shaykh 'Alī Ibn Nāsir al-Faqīhi (حفظه الله).

TRANSLITERATION TABLE

Consonants

ء	’	د	d	ض	ḍ	ك	k
ب	b	ذ	dh	ط	ṭ	ل	l
ت	t	ر	r	ظ	ẓ	م	m
ث	th	ز	z	ع	‘	ن	n
ج	j	س	s	غ	gh	هـ	h
ح	ḥ	ش	sh	ف	f	و	w
خ	kh	ص	ṣ	ق	q	ي	y

Vowels

Short	ـَ	a	ـِ	i	ـُ	u
Long	ـَا	ā	ـِي	ī	ـُو	ū

Diphthongs	ـَوْ	aw	ـَيْ	ay

Arabic Symbols & their meanings

حفظه الله	May Allāh preserve him
رَضِيَ ٱللَّهُ عَنْهُ	May Allāh be pleased with him (i.e. a male companion of the Prophet Muḥammad)
سُبْحَانَهُ وَتَعَالَىٰ	Glorified & Exalted is Allāh
عَزَّ وَجَلَّ	(Allāh) the Mighty & Sublime
تَبَارَكَ وَتَعَالَىٰ	(Allāh) the Blessed & Exalted
جَلَّ وَعَلَا	(Allāh) the Sublime & Exalted
عَلَيْهِ ٱلصَّلَاةُ وَٱلسَّلَامُ	May Allāh send Blessings & Safety upon him (i.e. a Prophet or Messenger)
صَلَّى ٱللَّهُ عَلَيْهِ وَعَلَىٰ آلِهِ وَسَلَّمَ	May Allāh send Blessings & Safety upon him and his family (i.e. Du'ā sent when mentioning the Prophet Muḥammad)

رَحِمَهُ ٱللَّهُ	May Allāh have mercy upon him
رَضِيَ ٱللَّهُ عَنْهُمْ	May Allāh be pleased with them (i.e. Du'ā made for the Companions of the Prophet Muḥammad)
جَلَّ جَلَالُهُ	(Allāh) His Majesty is Exalted
رَضِيَ ٱللَّهُ عَنْهَا	May Allāh be pleased with her (i.e. a female companion of the Prophet Muḥammad)

INTRODUCTION

Indeed, all praise belongs to Allāh. We praise Him; we seek His assistance and forgiveness. We seek refuge with Allāh from our evil selves and wicked actions. Whoever Allāh guides none can misguide him; and whoever has been led astray no one will be able to guide him.

I bear witness that none has the right to be worshiped, in truth, except Allāh alone who has no partners; and I bear witness that Muḥammad is His servant and final Messenger. May Allāh send abundant Ṣalāh and blessings upon him, his family, and all of his Companions.

To proceed:

The topic of this discussion is entitled **"Our Obligation Concerning the Noble Companions"** (May Allāh be pleased with them); which is an enormous duty and a great demand (by Islām) that is befitting for us all to peak our interest and devote the utmost concern.

The honored reader should also know that our obligation to the Companions is a part of our obligation to our religion; the religion of Islām which Allāh has approved for His servants. No other religion besides it will be accepted from them as Allāh says,

﴿ إِنَّ ٱلدِّينَ عِندَ ٱللَّهِ ٱلْإِسْلَـٰمُ ﴾

"Truly, the religion with Allāh is Islām." [*Sūrah ʿĀli ʿImrān* 3:19]

Likewise, Allāh says,

﴿ وَمَن يَبْتَغِ غَيْرَ ٱلْإِسْلَـٰمِ دِينًا فَلَن يُقْبَلَ مِنْهُ وَهُوَ فِى ٱلْـَٔاخِرَةِ مِنَ ٱلْخَـٰسِرِينَ ﴿٨٥﴾ ﴾

"And whoever seeks a religion other than Islām, it will never be accepted of him, and in the Hereafter, he will be one of the losers." [*Sūrah 'Āli 'Imrān* 3:85]

And Allāh says,

﴿ ٱلْيَوْمَ أَكْمَلْتُ لَكُمْ دِينَكُمْ وَأَتْمَمْتُ عَلَيْكُمْ نِعْمَتِي وَرَضِيتُ لَكُمُ ٱلْإِسْلَٰمَ دِينًا ﴾

"This day, I have perfected your religion for you, completed My Favor upon you, and have chosen for you Islām as your religion." [*Sūrah al-Mā'idah* 5:3]

This true religion and straight path is the religion of Allāh (عَزَّوَجَلَّ). Allāh selected a trustworthy Messenger; one who is a sincere advisor and wise;

an honored Messenger who is Muḥammad (صَلَّى ٱللَّهُ عَلَيْهِ وَسَلَّمَ).

He conveyed this religion in a complete manner, explained it fully, and established what His Lord (تَبَارَكَ وَتَعَالَىٰ) ordered in the most perfect aspect and circumstance. As Allāh ordered him,

﴿ ۞ يَٰٓأَيُّهَا ٱلرَّسُولُ بَلِّغْ مَآ أُنزِلَ إِلَيْكَ مِن رَّبِّكَ ۖ وَإِن لَّمْ تَفْعَلْ فَمَا بَلَّغْتَ رِسَالَتَهُۥ ۚ وَٱللَّهُ يَعْصِمُكَ مِنَ ٱلنَّاسِ ۗ إِنَّ ٱللَّهَ لَا يَهْدِى ٱلْقَوْمَ ٱلْكَٰفِرِينَ ﴿٦٧﴾ ﴾

"O Messenger (Muḥammad صَلَّى ٱللَّهُ عَلَيْهِ وَسَلَّمَ)! Proclaim (the Message) which has been sent down to you from your Lord. And if you do not, then you have not conveyed His Message. Allāh will protect you from humanity. Verily, Allāh guides not the

people who disbelieve." [*Sūrah al-Mā'idah 5:67*]

Hence, he conveyed the message, fulfilled the trust (given to him), sincerely advised the ʾUmmah, and strived in the path of Allāh until death reached him. No good was left out except that he directed the ʾUmmah to it; nor was any evil left out except that he warned against it.

Allāh (سُبْحَانَهُۥ وَتَعَالَىٰ) says, mentioning His favor and blessing upon His servants,

﴿ هُوَ ٱلَّذِى بَعَثَ فِى ٱلْأُمِّيِّـۧنَ رَسُولًا مِّنْهُمْ يَتْلُوا۟ عَلَيْهِمْ ءَايَـٰتِهِۦ وَيُزَكِّيهِمْ وَيُعَلِّمُهُمُ ٱلْكِتَـٰبَ وَٱلْحِكْمَةَ وَإِن كَانُوا۟ مِن قَبْلُ لَفِى ضَلَـٰلٍ مُّبِينٍ ۝٢ ﴾

"He it is Who sent among the unlettered ones a Messenger (Muḥammad صَلَّى ٱللَّهُ عَلَيْهِ وَسَلَّمَ)

from among themselves, reciting to them His Verses, purifying them (from the filth of disbelief and polytheism), and teaching them the Book (this Qur'ān, Islāmic laws and Islāmic jurisprudence) and *Al-Ḥikmah* (*As-Sunnah*: legal ways, orders, acts of worship, etc. of Prophet Muḥammad صَلَّىٱللَّهُعَلَيْهِوَسَلَّمَ). And verily, they had been before in manifest error." [*Sūrah al-Jumuʿah* 62:2]

Our Messenger (صَلَّىٱللَّهُعَلَيْهِوَسَلَّمَ) conveyed Allāh's religion in a complete and perfect fashion. He sincerely advised the ʾ Ummah, clarified for them the straight way, and made the correct path distinct.

Likewise, Allāh (جَلَّوَعَلَا) selected for this noble Messenger just supporters and faithful leaders who aided him & the religion of Allāh (تَبَارَكَوَتَعَالَىٰ).

They (رَضِيَ ٱللَّهُ عَنْهُمْ) were the best Companions for the best of whoever walked the face of the earth. They were dutiful Companions, honorable brethren, and strong supporters who aided Allāh's religion.

They were the best of supporters to spread and aid this religion. How delightful that they have been bestowed such an exalted and magnificent status! And how illustrious are the effort(s) they undertook to aid the religion of Allāh (تَبَارَكَ وَتَعَالَىٰ)!

Allāh (عَزَّ وَجَلَّ) selected these Companions for His Prophet (صَلَّى ٱللَّهُ عَلَيْهِ وَسَلَّمَ) based on His infinite knowledge and wisdom. He selected the best and most just. By the testament of the Lord of all that exists and that of the Noble Messenger (صَلَّى ٱللَّهُ عَلَيْهِ وَسَلَّمَ), the Companions were the best of humanity after the Prophets, just as Allāh (سُبْحَانَهُ وَتَعَالَىٰ) says,

﴿ كُنتُمْ خَيْرَ أُمَّةٍ أُخْرِجَتْ لِلنَّاسِ ﴾

"You [true believers in Islāmic Monotheism, and real followers of Prophet Muḥammad and his *Sunnah* (legal ways, etc.)] are the best of peoples ever raised up for mankind." [*Sūrah 'Ālī ʿImrān 3:110*]

The first to fall under this (statement) are the Companions of the Prophet (صَلَّىٱللَّهُعَلَيۡهِوَسَلَّمَ). They are firstly mentioned in this praise.

A Ḥadīth mentioned in the two Ṣaḥīḥ from the Prophet (صَلَّىٱللَّهُعَلَيۡهِوَسَلَّمَ) said,

خَيْرُ النَّاسِ قَرْنِي ، ثُمَّ الَّذِينَ يَلُونَهُمْ ، ثُمَّ الَّذِينَ يَلُونَهُمْ.

> **"The best of humanity is my generation, then those who follow them, then those who follow them."**[1]

This statement holds within it an act of beneficence to the Companions which the Lord of all that exists and His Noble Messenger (صَلَّى ٱللَّهُ عَلَيْهِ وَسَلَّمَ) acknowledge. They were outstanding, just, trusted, established leaders, and guides to the truth (رَضِيَ ٱللَّهُ عَنْهُمْ).

Based upon this, it becomes incumbent upon us to bear in mind that aḥādīth from the Companions (رَضِيَ ٱللَّهُ عَنْهُمْ), as well as what we are obliged concerning them, are a part of the religion, the Islāmic Creed, and the ʾĪmān in which we worship Allāh (تَبَارَكَ وَتَعَالَىٰ) with.

---

[1] Collected by al-Bukhārī (2652) and Muslim (2533) from the Ḥadīth of Ibn Masood (رَضِيَ ٱللَّهُ عَنْهُ).

So if you were to read the books of ʿAqīdah authored by the Imāms of the Salaf old and new, you will not find a single book that is devoid of clarifying the ʿAqīdah concerning the Companions.

WHY IS THE OBLIGATION CONCERNING THE COMPANIONS A PART OF OUR OBLIGATION CONCERNING OUR RELIGION?

So the question that one should pose to himself is:

"Why is the obligation concerning the Companions a part of our obligation concerning our religion?"

I say, the Companions (رَضِيَ ٱللَّهُ عَنْهُمْ) are carriers of this religion and those who conveyed it to the 'Ummah. Allāh (سُبْحَانَهُ وَتَعَالَىٰ) conferred honor and dignity to them by allowing them to hear this religion from the Messenger of Allāh (صَلَّىٰ ٱللَّهُ عَلَيْهِ وَسَلَّمَ); and likewise, Allāh conferred honor to them by allowing them to see him (صَلَّىٰ ٱللَّهُ عَلَيْهِ وَسَلَّمَ) and to hear the aḥādīth from him without intermediaries.

They saw him, listened to him, memorized, understood him and conveyed it to the ʾUmmah of Islām.

Is there present a single narration of the Prophet (صَلَّىٱللَّهُعَلَيۡهِوَسَلَّمَ)—whether in speech or action—that reached us from other than the Companions?!

If you were to open (read) the books of Ḥadīth like Ṣaḥīḥ al-Bukhārī, Ṣaḥīḥ Muslim, as-Sunan, Masānīd, or the books of Jāmiʿ, you would find the chain of narrators starting from the author, in which he states,

> **"Such-and-such person narrated to us, from such-and-such person until it reaches the Companion; then the Companion narrates (directly) from the Prophet (صَلَّىٱللَّهُعَلَيۡهِوَسَلَّمَ)."**

So all aḥādīth which have been graded authentic and affirmed from the Messenger of Allāh

(صَلَّىٰ ٱللَّهُ عَلَيْهِ وَسَلَّمَ) their chain of narrators to the Prophet (صَلَّىٰ ٱللَّهُ عَلَيْهِ وَسَلَّمَ) has a noble Companion in it.

THE INTEGRITY OF THE COMPANIONS

The Companions (رَضِيَ ٱللَّهُ عَنْهُمْ), all of them are just. Allāh (جَلَّ وَعَلَا) and His Prophet (صَلَّى ٱللَّهُ عَلَيْهِ وَسَلَّمَ) called them just and validated their trustworthiness in His Book. And based upon this, the way of the Imāms of the Salaf and the scholars of the Sunnah in aḥādīth which were transmitted from the Prophet (صَلَّى ٱللَّهُ عَلَيْهِ وَسَلَّمَ) proceeded by researching the integrity of narrators and their status, whether they were trustworthy or weak. They would research the circumstance of every narrator in the Isnād (i.e., a chain of narrators in a Ḥadīth) - is he trustworthy or not; is he just or not - up until the Isnād reaches a Companion; because the Companions (رَضِيَ ٱللَّهُ عَنْهُمْ) are just and trustworthy.

Based upon this, when you read the books of 'Ilal and books on the science of men, those books begin at the time of the second generation of Muslims and then after them. You find in every one of them there is speech about their circumstance.

They would say, "such-and-such is trustworthy, such-and-such is firm, such-and-such is a Hafiz, such-and-such is weak, and such-and-such is like this, except the Companions. Not a single scholar spoke about them—are they (i.e., Companions) just or not; are they trustworthy or not.

The reason for that is that the integrity of all of them has been vouched for by the Lord of all that exists (جَلَّ وَعَلَا), as well as by His Messenger (صَلَّى ٱللَّهُ عَلَيْهِ وَسَلَّمَ). This is noted in numerous verses in the Qur'ān and in many aḥādīth of the Noble Messenger (صَلَّى ٱللَّهُ عَلَيْهِ وَسَلَّمَ).

THE COMPANIONS ARE THE CONVEYERS OF THIS RELIGION

The Companions (رَضِيَ ٱللَّهُ عَنْهُمْ) are the conveyers of this religion. They heard it from the Messenger of Allāh (صَلَّى ٱللَّهُ عَلَيْهِ وَسَلَّمَ) They memorized and preserved it just as they heard it and then they conveyed it to the ʾUmmah with all surety and trustworthiness. Every one of them said, "This is what we heard from the Messenger of Allāh (صَلَّى ٱللَّهُ عَلَيْهِ وَسَلَّمَ) and we will convey it to you completely as we heard it."

These Companions earned an abundant and full reward from the Prophet's (صَلَّى ٱللَّهُ عَلَيْهِ وَسَلَّمَ) supplication when he said,

نَضَّرَ اللهُ امْرَأً سَمِعَ مِنَّا حَدِيثاً فَحَفِظَهُ حَتَّى يُبَلِّغَهُ.

"May Allāh cause the person to shine whoever hears from me a Ḥadīth, memorizes it and then conveys it."[2]

So do you know of anyone from this ʾUmmah who, with regards to this tremendous supplication, will reach a level of success that is equal to the Companions (رَضِيَٱللَّهُعَنْهُمْ)?

They preserved the religion with the aḥādīth of the Noble Messenger (صَلَّىٱللَّهُعَلَيْهِوَسَلَّمَ). Then they conveyed it to the ʾUmmah in its pure and complete form with all trustworthiness; with acute precision and care. So in this fashion, was the case of the Companions (رَضِيَٱللَّهُعَنْهُمْ).

They were eager to sit in the company of the Prophet (صَلَّىٱللَّهُعَلَيْهِوَسَلَّمَ) and compete in attending and

---

[2]Collected by Abū Dāwud (3662), at-Tirmidhī (2656), and Ibn Mājah (230) from the Ḥadīth Zayd ibn Thābit who reported it from a group of the Companions with similar wording. Shaykh al-Albānī graded it to be Ṣaḥīḥ (404).

listening to the aḥādīth, memorizing them, retaining them within their hearts, and delivering them to the ʾUmmah of Islām.

AḤĀDĪTH FROM THE COMPANIONS (رَضِيَ ٱللَّهُ عَنْهُمْ) ARE AḤĀDĪTH FROM THE RELIGION

Since the Companions (رَضِيَ ٱللَّهُ عَنْهُمْ) are on this outstanding and dignified level, then aren't the aḥādīth from them a portion of the aḥādīth of the religion? Since they are carriers and transmitters (of the religion) to the 'Ummah, every Ḥadīth from them is a Ḥadīth about this religion.

LODGING CRITICISM AGAINST THE COMPANIONS IS DOING SO AGAINST THE RELIGION

Equally so, lodging criticism against them (رَضِيَ اللَّهُ عَنْهُمْ) is doing so against the religion itself, just as the scholars of Islām have stated,

> **"Lodging criticism against a narrator is doing so against what is being narrated."**

If the ones relaying to us the religion are the Companions (رَضِيَ اللَّهُ عَنْهُمْ) and they are being defamed; their integrity is being talked about, as well as their trustworthiness, then what is the case concerning the religion if the one being defamed concerning the religion is the same (one) who is transmitting to us the religion? – Then the religion itself is defamed.

Based upon this, the Imām, al-Ḥāfiẓ Abū Zurah ar-Rāzī (رَحِمَهُ ٱللَّهُ) stated,

> **"If you see a man disparaging one of the Companions of the Prophet (صَلَّى ٱللَّهُ عَلَيْهِ وَسَلَّمَ) understand that this person is a heretic and the Messenger (صَلَّى ٱللَّهُ عَلَيْهِ وَسَلَّمَ) before us is the truth; the Qur'ān is true; and the Companions of the Messenger (صَلَّى ٱللَّهُ عَلَيْهِ وَسَلَّمَ) are the only (ones) who conveyed to us the Qur'ān and Sunnah; and these individuals wish to discredit our testimony in order to invalidate the Qur'ān and Sunnah. So criticizing them is more suitable because they are heretics."**[3]

[3] Al-Kifāyah fi 'Ilm ar-Riwayah, authored by al-Khateeb al-Baghdādī (page 49).

If the Companions (رَضِيَ ٱللَّهُ عَنْهُمْ) were untrustworthy and unjust, where would the religion in which we worship Allāh with be?

A group of people plunge into misguidance and start reviling all of the Companions except for a small group of which can be counted on the hands.

It is said to them, "If this matter has this condition, then where is the religion?! How will Allāh's religion be learned and understood?! How will Allāh be worshiped?! How will Allāh be prayed and prostrated to?! How will the religious obligations be performed?! How will Ḥajj be performed at House (i.e., the Ka'bah)?! How will obedience to Him be performed?! How will the prohibitions be abstained from when the Companions of the Prophet (عَلَيْهِ ٱلصَّلَاةُ وَٱلسَّلَامُ) are disparaged in what they transmitted and carried (of the religion)."

Based upon this, we need to understand that disparaging the ones who transmitted the religion, who are the Companions, is disparaging the religion itself. We need to understand fully (as well) that our obligation towards the Companions is a part of our obligation towards our religion, because they are the ones who transmitted it. So when they are disparaged the religion is disparaged too.

How are they disparaged while the Lord of all that exists described them as being veracious in many verses of His Clear Book? Rather, Allāh (جَلَّ وَعَلَا) informed us that He is pleased with them and they are pleased with Him.

Allāh (سُبۡحَانَهُۥ وَتَعَالَىٰ) says,

﴿ وَٱلسَّٰبِقُونَ ٱلۡأَوَّلُونَ مِنَ ٱلۡمُهَٰجِرِينَ وَٱلۡأَنصَارِ وَٱلَّذِينَ ٱتَّبَعُوهُم بِإِحۡسَٰنٖ رَّضِيَ ٱللَّهُ عَنۡهُمۡ وَرَضُواْ عَنۡهُ ﴾

"And the first to embrace Islām of the *Muhājirūn* (those who migrated from Makkah to Al-Madīnah) and the Ansār (the citizens of Al-Madīnah who helped and gave aid to the *Muhājirūn*) and also those who followed them exactly (in Faith). Allāh

is well-pleased with them as they are well-pleased with Him." **[*Sūrah at-Tawbah 9:100*]**

Allāh (جَلَّ وَعَلَا) informed us that He is pleased with them; so is Allāh pleased with someone who is not trustworthy in what they transmit?! Is Allāh (جَلَّ وَعَلَا) pleased with someone who betrayed the delivery of what the Noble Messenger said (عَلَيْهِ ٱلصَّلَاةُ وَٱلسَّلَامُ)?! This is absurd! Never!

Allāh is pleased with them because they are trustworthy and just, because they are leaders in excellence and because they conveyed Allāh's religion in the most complete and excellent manner. As He states,

﴿ رَّضِيَ ٱللَّهُ عَنْهُمْ وَرَضُوا۟ عَنْهُ ﴾

"Allāh is well-pleased with them as they are well-pleased with Him."

Allāh (سُبْحَانَهُوَتَعَالَىٰ) says in another verse,

﴿ ۞ لَّقَدْ رَضِيَ ٱللَّهُ عَنِ ٱلْمُؤْمِنِينَ إِذْ يُبَايِعُونَكَ تَحْتَ ٱلشَّجَرَةِ ﴾

> **"Indeed, Allāh was pleased with the believers when they gave their *Bai'a* (pledge) to you (O Muḥammad صَلَّىٱللَّهُعَلَيْهِوَسَلَّمَ) under the tree." [*Sūrah al-Fatḥ 48:18*]**

Their number exceeded more than a thousand and Allāh is pleased with all of them. He (صَلَّىٱللَّهُعَلَيْهِوَسَلَّمَ) said about the people who fought in Badr,

وَ مَا يُدْرِيكَ لَعَلَّ اللهَ أَنْ يَكُونَ قَدِ اطَّلَعَ عَلَى أَهْلِ بَدْرٍ فَقَالَ : اِعْمَلُوا مَا شِئْتُمْ ؛ فَقَدْ غَفَرْتُ لَكُمْ

> **"And what do you know, perhaps Allāh might look with pity on those who were present at Badr? And said, "Do what you wish, I have forgiven you."**[4]

This statement is a commendation, one after another, and a praise, one after another, which is a tremendous laudation recurrent throughout the Noble Qur'ān and the Sunnah of the Prophet (صَلَّىٰ اللَّهُ عَلَيْهِ وَسَلَّمَ). The verses and narrations concerning the laudation of the Companions (رَضِيَ اللَّهُ عَنْهُمْ) cannot even be enumerated.

Laudation of the Companions (رَضِيَ اللَّهُ عَنْهُمْ), not only is mentioned in the Qur'ān; rather, laudation of them came before their existence on the earth. Their praise was mentioned in the Old and New Testaments (i.e., Torah & Injīl) before their creation

---

[4] Collected by al-Bukhārī (3007) and Muslim (2494) from the Ḥadīth of Alī (رَضِيَ اللَّهُ عَنْهُ).

and existence. Within the last verse of Sūrah al-Fatḥ, Allāh says about the Companions (رَضِيَ ٱللَّهُ عَنْهُمْ),

﴿ مُّحَمَّدٌ رَّسُولُ ٱللَّهِ ۚ وَٱلَّذِينَ مَعَهُۥٓ أَشِدَّآءُ عَلَى ٱلْكُفَّارِ رُحَمَآءُ بَيْنَهُمْ ۖ تَرَىٰهُمْ رُكَّعًا سُجَّدًا يَبْتَغُونَ فَضْلًا مِّنَ ٱللَّهِ وَرِضْوَٰنًا ۖ سِيمَاهُمْ فِى وُجُوهِهِم مِّنْ أَثَرِ ٱلسُّجُودِ ۚ ﴾

"Muḥammad (صَلَّى ٱللَّهُ عَلَيْهِ وَسَلَّمَ) is the Messenger of Allāh, and those who are with him are severe against disbelievers, and merciful among themselves. You see them bowing and falling prostrate (in prayer), seeking Bounty from Allāh and (His) Good Pleasure. The mark of them (i.e. of their Faith) is on their faces (foreheads) from the traces of (their) prostration (during prayers)." [*Sūrah al-Fatḥ 48:29*]

So the Lord (عَزَّوَجَلَّ) praises the Companions; hence where is this example and in which book is it found? Allāh (سُبْحَانَهُۥوَتَعَالَىٰ) says,

﴿ ذَٰلِكَ مَثَلُهُمْ فِي ٱلتَّوْرَىٰةِ ۚ وَمَثَلُهُمْ فِي ٱلْإِنجِيلِ كَزَرْعٍ أَخْرَجَ شَطْـَٔهُۥ فَـَٔازَرَهُۥ فَٱسْتَغْلَظَ فَٱسْتَوَىٰ عَلَىٰ سُوقِهِۦ يُعْجِبُ ٱلزُّرَّاعَ لِيَغِيظَ بِهِمُ ٱلْكُفَّارَ ۗ وَعَدَ ٱللَّهُ ٱلَّذِينَ ءَامَنُوا۟ وَعَمِلُوا۟ ٱلصَّـٰلِحَـٰتِ مِنْهُم مَّغْفِرَةً وَأَجْرًا عَظِيمًۢا ﴿٢٩﴾ ﴾

"This is their description in the Taurat (Torah). But their description in the Injīl (Gospel) is like a (sown) seed which sends forth its shoot, then makes it strong, it then becomes thick, and it stands straight on its stem, delighting the sowers that He may enrage the disbelievers with them. Allāh has promised those among them who

believe (i.e. all those who follow Islāmic Monotheism, the religion of Prophet Muḥammad صَلَّى ٱللَّهُ عَلَيْهِ وَسَلَّمَ till the Day of Resurrection) and do righteous good deeds, forgiveness and a mighty reward (i.e. Paradise)." [*Sūrah al-Fatḥ 48:29*]

This sweet-smelling praise of these honored Companions (رَضِيَ ٱللَّهُ عَنْهُمْ) is mentioned in the Torah and Injīl.

This noble verse will clarify to you, my Muslim brother, that the All-Mighty Lord (i.e., Allāh) has praised the Companions, attested to their truthfulness and integrity in the Torah, the Injīl, and the Qur'ān.

It is a great and magnificent praise, and a lofty pronouncement of the credibility of these excellent individuals and just leaders.

Allāh has praised them even before their existence; and commended them before they were created when He revealed the Torah to Mūsā (عَلَيْهِ ٱلصَّلَاةُ وَٱلسَّلَامُ) and also when He revealed His Book, the Injīl, to Īsa (عَلَيْهِ ٱلصَّلَاةُ وَٱلسَّلَامُ); then He praised them while they were on the face of the Earth in the Noble Qur'ān which was revealed to Muḥammad (صَلَّى ٱللَّهُ عَلَيْهِ وَسَلَّمَ).

We read (also) another praise of the Companions (رَضِيَ ٱللَّهُ عَنْهُمْ) from the Lord of all that exists in Sūrah al-Ḥashr where Allāh (جَلَّ وَعَلَا) says,

﴿ لِلْفُقَرَآءِ ٱلْمُهَٰجِرِينَ ٱلَّذِينَ أُخْرِجُوا۟ مِن دِيَٰرِهِمْ وَأَمْوَٰلِهِمْ يَبْتَغُونَ فَضْلًا مِّنَ ٱللَّهِ وَرِضْوَٰنًا وَيَنصُرُونَ ٱللَّهَ وَرَسُولَهُۥٓ ۚ أُو۟لَٰٓئِكَ هُمُ ٱلصَّٰدِقُونَ ﴿٨﴾ ﴾

"(And there is also a share in this booty) for the poor emigrants, who were expelled from

their homes and their property, seeking Bounties from Allāh and to please Him. And helping Allāh (i.e. helping His religion) and His Messenger (Muḥammad صَلَّى ٱللَّهُ عَلَيْهِ وَسَلَّمَ). Such are indeed truthful (to what they say)." [*Sūrah al-Ḥashr 59:8*]

So Allāh (سُبْحَانَهُ وَتَعَالَىٰ) describes them in His statement as being **"Such are indeed the truthful"** then He says about al-Anṣār,

﴿ وَٱلَّذِينَ تَبَوَّءُو ٱلدَّارَ وَٱلْإِيمَٰنَ مِن قَبْلِهِمْ يُحِبُّونَ مَنْ هَاجَرَ إِلَيْهِمْ ﴾

"And those who, before them, had homes (in Al-Madīnah) and had adopted the Faith, love those who emigrate to them" [*Sūrah al-Ḥashr 59:9*]

Meaning that they loved those who migrated to Madīnah. Then Allāh continues,

﴿ وَلَا يَجِدُونَ فِي صُدُورِهِمْ حَاجَةً مِّمَّآ أُوتُوا۟ وَيُؤْثِرُونَ عَلَىٰٓ أَنفُسِهِمْ وَلَوْ كَانَ بِهِمْ خَصَاصَةٌ ۚ وَمَن يُوقَ شُحَّ نَفْسِهِۦ فَأُو۟لَٰٓئِكَ هُمُ ٱلْمُفْلِحُونَ ٩ ﴾

"and have no jealousy in their breasts for that which they have been given (from the booty of Banī An-Naḍīr), and give them (emigrants) preference over themselves, even though they were in need of that. And whosoever is saved from his own covetousness; such are they who will be successful." [*Sūrah al-Ḥashr 59:9*]

This statement is a praise to those who migrated to Madīnah as well as al-Anṣār, and it is no secret that the Companions are of two categories.

8.a.i.1. Those who migrated from Makkah.

8.a.i.2. And al-Anṣār.

The Muhājirūn are the people of Makkah who left their wealth and homes and migrated while seeking Allāh's face as stated,

﴿ يَبۡتَغُونَ فَضۡلٗا مِّنَ ٱللَّهِ وَرِضۡوَٰنٗا وَيَنصُرُونَ ٱللَّهَ وَرَسُولَهُۥٓۚ ﴾

"Seeking Bounties from Allāh and to please Him. And helping Allāh (i.e. helping His religion) and His Messenger (Muḥammad صَلَّىٱللَّهُعَلَيۡهِوَسَلَّمَ)." [*Sūrah al-Ḥashr 59:8*]

So, they left everything behind and went to Madīnah to aid Allāh and His Messenger. Allāh says about them, **"Such are indeed the truthful"** meaning that they were truthful in their ʾĪmān, companionship (of the Prophet), and their obedience and adherence to the religion of Allāh (تَبَارَكَ وَتَعَالَىٰ).

Allāh (سُبْحَانَهُ وَتَعَالَىٰ) says,

﴿ مِّنَ ٱلْمُؤْمِنِينَ رِجَالٌ صَدَقُوا۟ مَا عَـٰهَدُوا۟ ٱللَّهَ عَلَيْهِ ۖ فَمِنْهُم مَّن قَضَىٰ نَحْبَهُۥ وَمِنْهُم مَّن يَنتَظِرُ ۖ وَمَا بَدَّلُوا۟ تَبْدِيلًا ﴿٢٣﴾ ﴾

"Among the believers are men who have been true to their covenant with Allāh [i.e. they have gone out for *Jihād* (holy fighting), and showed not their backs to the disbelievers], of them some have fulfilled

their obligations (i.e. have been martyred), and some of them are still waiting, but they have never changed [i.e. they never proved treacherous to their covenant which they concluded with Allāh] in the least." [*Sūrah al-Ahzāb 33:23*]

These were the Companions (رَضِيَ ٱللَّهُ عَنْهُمْ) whom the Lord (جَلَّ وَعَلَا) gave this blessed and sweet-smelling praise to.

Just as Allāh (سُبْحَانَهُ وَتَعَالَىٰ) praised the Muhājirūn, He did so to al-Ansār. He says, **"And those who, before them, had homes"** what is intended here is Madīnah. The Ansār had provided accommodations (i.e. the city of Madīnah) before the Muhājirūn arrived. However, what exactly did al-Ansār do for the Muhājirūn upon their arrival? They gave up half of what they owned. The Ansārī gave half of his house and wealth to the Muhājir.

This act of selflessness is what Allāh praises in this verse,

﴿ وَيُؤْثِرُونَ عَلَىٰٓ أَنفُسِهِمْ وَلَوْ كَانَ بِهِمْ خَصَاصَةٌ ﴾

"And give them (emigrants) preference over themselves, even though they were in need of that."

The Ansār and al-Muhājirūn came together to aid and support the religion of Allāh (تَبَارَكَ وَتَعَالَىٰ). So all of them are essentially those who aided and supported Allāh's religion, **"but they have never changed in the least."**[5]

[5]Sūrah al-Ahzāb 33:23

THE CORRECT STANCE THE MUSLIM SHOULD HAVE REGARDING THE COMPANIONS

(رَضِيَ ٱللَّهُ عَنْهُمْ)

As previously outlined, this is their affair. So what is the affair of those who came after them—meaning the believers who followed them in excellence?

It is a must that we pay close attention here because of Allāh's (عَزَّوَجَلَّ) clarifying the methodology which is befitting for the believer to be upon with regards to the al-Muhājirūn and al-Ansār.

Allāh says,

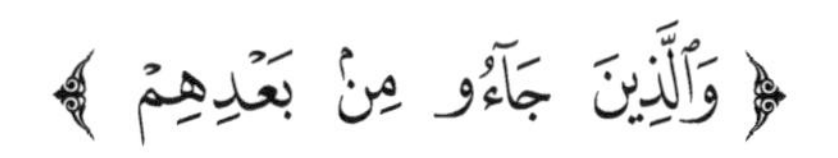

"And those who came after them." [*Sūrah al-Ḥashr 59:10*]

Meaning, after al-Muhājirūn and al-Anṣ ār. He continues,

﴿ يَقُولُونَ رَبَّنَا ٱغْفِرْ لَنَا وَلِإِخْوَٰنِنَا ٱلَّذِينَ سَبَقُونَا بِٱلْإِيمَٰنِ وَلَا تَجْعَلْ فِى قُلُوبِنَا غِلًّا لِّلَّذِينَ ءَامَنُوا۟ رَبَّنَآ إِنَّكَ رَءُوفٌ رَّحِيمٌ ﴿١٠﴾ ﴾

"Say: "Our Lord! Forgive us and our brethren who have preceded us in Faith, and put not in our hearts any hatred against those who have believed. Our Lord! You are indeed full of kindness, Most Merciful." [*Sūrah al-Ḥashr 59:10*]

This verse illustrates the methodology which is incumbent for every believer to be upon concerning the Companions (رَضِيَ ٱللَّهُ عَنْهُمْ). This obligation summarizes two affairs:

- **<u>The first affair</u>** is to be good-hearted towards the Companions (رَضِيَ ٱللَّهُ عَنْهُمْ); that our hearts are at peace regarding them, not a single bit of rancor, malice, spite, hatred, or enmity towards them. In their hearts, there should only be found love, beneficence, kindness, and friendship towards the Companions. We adopt this from Allāh's statement,

﴿ وَلَا تَجْعَلْ فِي قُلُوبِنَا غِلًّا لِّلَّذِينَ ءَامَنُوا۟ ﴾

"And put not in our hearts any hatred against those who have believed."

Meaning, we should condition our hearts to be good-hearted to those who have proceeded us in ʾĪmān (i.e., faith). They are not only our brethren, rather they are the most excellent of our brethren (رَضِيَ ٱللَّهُ عَنْهُمْ). So, based upon this Allāh says,

﴿ وَٱلَّذِينَ جَآءُو مِنۢ بَعۡدِهِمۡ يَقُولُونَ رَبَّنَا ٱغۡفِرۡ لَنَا وَلِإِخۡوَٰنِنَا ٱلَّذِينَ سَبَقُونَا بِٱلۡإِيمَٰنِ ﴾

"And those who came after them say: "Our Lord! Forgive us and our brethren who have preceded us in Faith."

So they are our brothers. In addition to that, they are highly distinguished and honored as Allāh mentions, **"Our brethren who have preceded us in Faith."**

And in another verse Allāh says,

﴿ وَٱلسَّٰبِقُونَ ٱلْأَوَّلُونَ مِنَ ٱلْمُهَٰجِرِينَ وَٱلْأَنصَارِ ﴾

"And the first to embrace Islām of the *Muhājirūn* (those who migrated from Makkah to Al-Madīnah) and the Ansār (the citizens of Al-Madīnah who helped and gave aid to the *Muhājirūn*)." [*Sūrah at-Tawbah 9:100*]

Allāh (جَلَّ وَعَلَا) mentions this statement to confer special honors upon them.

At present, we are in the fourteenth century and between them and us are several centuries; they were in the company of the Prophet (صَلَّى ٱللَّهُ عَلَيْهِ وَسَلَّمَ) when he was sent as a Prophet and Messenger and they aided, helped, and supported him—and they were with him side by side, so where are we in comparison to them!?

They preceded us in faith. They preceded us in aiding the religion. They preceded us in being dignified by Allāh (سُبْحَانَهُ وَتَعَالَىٰ) with being in the company of the Noble Prophet (صَلَّى ٱللَّهُ عَلَيْهِ وَسَلَّمَ), and based on that, you are ordered to make Du'ā for the Companions and are reminded of their precedence. This statement is a tremendous glance found in the verse when Allāh says,

﴿ رَبَّنَا ٱغْفِرْ لَنَا وَلِإِخْوَٰنِنَا ٱلَّذِينَ سَبَقُونَا بِٱلْإِيمَٰنِ ﴾

"They say: "Our Lord! Forgive us and our brethren who have preceded us in Faith."

They have rights over you regarding this great precedence. So, in order to know their worth, you must call to mind the precedence which Allāh (جَلَّ وَعَلَا) praises and commends them with, **"who have preceded us in Faith."**

What is to be understood is that the first matter is to be good-hearted towards the Companions, and we adopt this from Allāh's statement, **"and put not in our**

hearts any hatred against those who have believed."

The 2nd affair is to have a blameless tongue, meaning there are to be no insults, obscene language, execration or defamation towards them. Instead, there should only be supplications made for them. We take this position from Allāh's (سُبْحَانَهُ وَتَعَالَى) statement,

> **"They say: "Our Lord! Forgive us and our brethren who have preceded us in Faith."**

Did they (i.e., the believers who came after them) insult the Companions! Did they revile them?! Did they lodge criticism at them?! Did they defame their good repute?! Never! This isn't from the believers' nature; rather their character was just as Allāh says,

﴿ وَٱلَّذِينَ جَآءُو مِنۢ بَعۡدِهِمۡ يَقُولُونَ رَبَّنَا ٱغۡفِرۡ لَنَا وَلِإِخۡوَٰنِنَا ٱلَّذِينَ سَبَقُونَا بِٱلۡإِيمَٰنِ وَلَا تَجۡعَلۡ فِي قُلُوبِنَا غِلّٗا لِّلَّذِينَ ءَامَنُواْ رَبَّنَآ إِنَّكَ رَءُوفٞ رَّحِيمٌ ١٠ ﴾

"And those who came after them say: "Our Lord! Forgive us and our brethren who have preceded us in Faith, and put not in our hearts any hatred against those who have believed. Our Lord! You are indeed full of kindness, Most Merciful." [*Sūrah al-Ḥashr 59:10*]

Based upon this the methodology of the people of ʾĪmān towards the Companions (رَضِيَ ٱللَّهُ عَنْهُمْ) is summarized into two points:

1. Good-heartedness
2. Blameless tongue

Indeed, this is a clean heart and a pure tongue towards the Noble Companions (رَضِيَ ٱللَّهُ عَنْهُمْ).

THE VIRTUE OF THE COMPANIONS AND INVIOLABILITY OF INSULTING THEM

It is mentioned in two Sahīh (Bukhārī and Muslim) a ḥadīth from the Prophet (صَلَّى ٱللَّهُ عَلَيْهِ وَسَلَّمَ) in which he warns the ʾUmmah against insulting the Companions and at the same time he clarifies their status. He (عَلَيْهِ ٱلصَّلَاةُ وَٱلسَّلَامُ) said,

لَا تَسُبُّوا أَصْحَابِي ؛ فَوَالَّذِي نَفْسِي بِيَدِهِ لَوْ أَنْفَقَ أَحَدُكُمْ مِثْلَ أُحَدٍ ذَهَبًا مَا بَلَغَ مُدَّ أَحَدِهِمْ وَ لَا نَصِيفَهُ

"Do not revile my Companions, by Him in Whose Hand is my life, if one amongst you would have spent as much gold as 'Uḥud it

would not amount to as much as one *mudd* on behalf of one of them or half of it."[6]

If one of the Companions (رَضِيَ ٱللَّهُ عَنْهُمْ) were to give a mudd of food in charity to a poor person and you were to give gold the size of Mount 'Uḥud—which none of us is able to do so— in charity; or perhaps if one was able to bring forth gold the size of Mount 'Uḥud then surely he would be tried by it, become devoted to it, and become stingy with it (i.e. the wealth). Let's assume that one of us has gold the size of Mount 'Uḥud and gives it in charity it wouldn't even reach a mudd of one of the Companions. So pay close attention and understand the value and status of the Companions (رَضِيَ ٱللَّهُ عَنْهُمْ).

---

[6]Collected by al-Bukhārī (3673) from the ḥadīth of Abū Said al-Khudri (رَضِيَ ٱللَّهُ عَنْهُ); and Muslim (2540) from the ḥadīth of Abū Hurayrah (رَضِيَ ٱللَّهُ عَنْهُ).

"Don't revile my Companions." This is the statement from the Prophet's speech (عَلَيْهِ ٱلصَّلَاةُ وَٱلسَّلَامُ)—not the speech of any person or scholar; rather it is the speech of the Messenger (صَلَّى ٱللَّهُ عَلَيْهِ وَسَلَّمَ) advising the ʾUmmah and warning them against disparaging any one of the Companions or degrading anyone of them (رَضِيَ ٱللَّهُ عَنْهُمْ); and he stresses the importance of knowing their value and status.

The aḥādīth of the Prophet (صَلَّى ٱللَّهُ عَلَيْهِ وَسَلَّمَ) on this matter are numerous. Within these aḥādīth, he clarifies to the ʾUmmah the affair of the Companions, their status and value, as well as their outstanding qualities. When some of the scholars want to single out the outstanding qualities of the Companions in one book, they aren't able to gather it into just one volume; rather they will need volumes and volumes due to the copious affirmed aḥādīth of the Prophet

(صَلَّى ٱللَّهُ عَلَيْهِ وَسَلَّمَ) pertaining to praising the Companions individually as well as collectively.

Look at how exalted is their worth and how momentous is their status; and how sublime is their rank; and how great is the Muslims' obligation concerning them (رَضِيَ ٱللَّهُ عَنْهُمْ).

Allāh (سُبْحَانَهُ وَتَعَالَىٰ) orders the people of ʾĪmān to make Du'ā for the Companions and seek forgiveness for them and they have done so. However, some people do the opposite of what they were commanded and turn it upside down. They do the exact opposite of what the Qur'ān and the Sunnah of the Prophet (صَلَّى ٱللَّهُ عَلَيْهِ وَسَلَّمَ) requires them.

So they exchange seeking forgiveness with insults. They exchange praise with lodging criticism. And based upon this, it is mentioned in Sahīh Muslim[7] that ʿĀishah (رَضِيَٱللَّهُعَنْهَا) said to ʻUrwa bin az-Zubayr,

يَا ابْنَ أُخْتِي! أُمِرُوا أَنْ يَسْتَغْفِرُوا لِأَصْحَابِ النَّبِيِّ صَلَّى اللهُ عَلَيْهِ وَ سَلَّمَ فَسَبُّوهُمْ.

"O my dear nephew! They were ordered to seek forgiveness for the Companions of the Prophet (صَلَّىٱللَّهُعَلَيْهِوَسَلَّمَ), and instead, they insulted them."

Yet within this matter divine wisdom belongs to Allāh (سُبْحَانَهُۥوَتَعَالَىٰ). ʿĀishah (رَضِيَٱللَّهُعَنْهَا) says as Ibn al-'Athīr mentioned in his book *Jāmi al-Usūl*[8] on the authority of Jābir ibn ʻAbdullāh (رَضِيَٱللَّهُعَنْهُمَا) said,

[7]Collected by Muslim (#3022)

[8](#6366) although he doesn't cite the *takhrīj*; Ibn Asaakir collected it in his Musnad in the book *Tarīkh Damashaq* (44/387); and al-Khatīb al-Baghdādī collected it in his book *Tarīkh Baghdad* (5/147).

إِنَّ نَاسًا يَتَنَاوَلُونَ أَصْحَابَ النَّبِيِّ صَلَّى اللهُ عَلَيْهِ وَ سَلَّمَ ، حَتَّى أَبَا بَكْرٍ وَ عُمَرَ ، فَقَالَتْ : وَ مَا تَعْجَبُونَ مِنْ هَذَا ؟ اِنْقَطَعَ عَنْهُمُ الْعَمَلُ ، فَأَحَبَّ اللهُ أَنْ لَا يَقْطَعَ عَنْهُمُ الْأَجْرَ .

"It was said to ʿĀishah, 'Indeed the people disparaged the Companions of the Prophet (ﷺ), even Abū Bakr and ʿUmar.' ʿĀishah said, 'What are you surprised about? Their good deeds have been severed from them; Allāh likes their (Companions) reward not to be cut off.'"

How is this!? We know with clear knowledge from the Sunnah that whoever unjustly lodges criticism at others or (someone else) he will have his good deeds taken; meaning the good deeds of the critic, and they will be given to the one being unjustly criticized as is (mentioned) in the ḥadīth of the bankrupt person. So you can understand what will occur on the Day of Resurrection to the one who lodges criticism at the Companions. The Prophet (ﷺ) said to the Companions one day,

إِنَّ الْمُفْلِسَ مِنْ أُمَّتِي يَأْتِي يَوْمَ الْقِيَامَةِ بِصَلَاةٍ وَ صِيَامٍ وَ زَكَاةٍ، وَ يَأْتِي قَدْ شَتَمَ هَذَا، وَ قَذَفَ هَذَا ، وَ أَكَلَ مَالَ هَذَا، وَ سَفَكَ دَمَ هَذَا، وَ ضَرَبَ هَذَا، فَيُعْطَى هَذَا مِنْ حَسَنَاتِهِ، وَ هَذَا مِنْ حَسَنَاتِهِ، فَإِنْ فَنِيَتْ حَسَنَاتُهُ قَبْلَ أَنْ يُقْضَى مَا عَلَيْهِ أُخِذَ مِنْ خَطَايَاهُمْ فَطُرِحَتْ عَلَيْهِ ثُمَّ طُرِحَ فِي النَّارِ

"The poor of my ʾUmmah would be he who would come on the Day of Resurrection

with prayers and fasts and Zakāh but (he would find himself bankrupt on that day as he would have exhausted his funds of virtues) since he hurled abuses upon others, brought calumny against others and unlawfully consumed the wealth of others and shed the blood of others and beat others, and his virtues would be credited to the account of one (who suffered at his hand). And if his good deeds fall short to clear the account, then his sins would be entered in (his account) and he would be thrown in the Hell-Fire."[9]

We ask Allāh for well-being and safety. As this (what was mentioned in the ḥadīth) pertains to the one who insults the Companions of the Noble Prophet (صَلَّىٱللَّهُعَلَيْهِوَسَلَّمَ), surely that is the greatest

[9]Collected by Muslim (2581) from the ḥadīth of Abū Hurayrah (رَضِيَٱللَّهُعَنْهُ).

calamity and more severe disaster! When this person who insulted the Companions comes on the day of Resurrection, his good deeds will be taken and given to the Noble Companions, and if his good deeds came to an end then the bad deeds of the one who was disparaged are taken and are flung at the disparager. Then he will be thrown into the Hellfire. How terrible of a calamity for whoever disparages the Companions!

And how severe is his trial/affliction and how heinous is his disaster when he comes on the day of Resurrection bankrupt?! Abū Bakr (رَضِيَ ٱللَّهُ عَنْهُ) will take from him good deeds. ʿUmar (رَضِيَ ٱللَّهُ عَنْهُ) will take from his good deeds. The wives of the Prophet (صَلَّى ٱللَّهُ عَلَيْهِ وَسَلَّمَ) will take from his good deeds, and in the same fashion, so will the rest of the Noble Companions (رَضِيَ ٱللَّهُ عَنْهُمْ).

What is amazing is that the Mother of the Believers, ʿĀishah (رَضِيَٱللَّهُعَنۡهَا) was not free from their criticism despite Allāh absolving her in the Qur'ān from what the people of lies and falsehood accused her of; Allāh sent down this absolution in verses of Sūrah an-Nūr which are recited concerning waging war against the Muslims until the Day of Resurrection. Still, there are individuals who lodge criticism against her. So what will ʿĀishah have on the Day of Resurrection? It will be an enormous share of good deeds. Afterwards, these people who criticized her will come on the Day of Resurrection bankrupt because they dedicated themselves to being constant criticizers and execrations against the Companions of the Prophet (صَلَّىٱللَّهُعَلَيۡهِوَسَلَّمَ). Some people criticize and execrate the Companions of the Messenger of Allāh (صَلَّىٱللَّهُعَلَيۡهِوَسَلَّمَ) day and night – and Allāh's refuge is sought. So how will their circumstance be on the Day of Resurrection when they meet Allāh (جَلَّ وَعَلَا)?!

Some of them even say, *"O Allāh curse the two idols of Quraysh, their two false gods, their two daughters (i.e. Abū Bakr & 'Umar)."* They say this in spite of the fact that the Prophet (صَلَّى ٱللَّهُ عَلَيْهِ وَسَلَّمَ) said concerning the affair of the believer in general:

لَيْسَ الْمُؤْمِنُ بِالطَّعَّانِ ، وَ لَا اللَّعَّانِ ، وَ لَا الْفَاحِشِ ، وَ لَا الْبَذِيءِ.

"A true believer is not involved in taunting, or frequently cursing (others) or in indecency or abusing."[10]

[10]Collected by Ahmad (3949); and al-Bukhārī in the book 'Adab-Mufrad (312); and at-Tirmidhī (1977); and al-Ḥākim (1/12) from the Ḥadīth of ibn Mas'ūd (رَضِيَ ٱللَّهُ عَنْهُ). At-Tirmidhī graded the Ḥadīth as Ḥasan Gharīb and al-Ḥākim said that is Ṣaḥīḥ upon the conditions of al-Bukhārī and Muslim; and adh-Dhahabī agreed

Rather, when the Prophet (صَلَّى ٱللَّٰهُ عَلَيْهِ وَسَلَّمَ) was asked, "O Messenger of Allāh! Supplicate against the Polytheists. He said, "Indeed, I was not sent for execration."

Afterward, a group of people who were forsaken selected the best of the ʾUmmah and most excellent to curse, and we seek refuge with Allāh from this abandonment.

---

and Shaykh al-Albānī graded it to be Ṣaḥīḥ in his book as-Saḥīḥah (312).

THE VARIOUS DEGREES OF VIRTUES AMONGST THE COMPANIONS

An authentic narration is mentioned from the Prophet (ﷺ) and reported by a number of Companions; among them Alī ibn Abū Tālib (رَضِيَ اللَّهُ عَنْهُ), in which he said,

قَالَ - عَلَيْهِ الصَّلَاةُ وَ السَّلَامُ - أَبُو بَكْرٍ وَ عُمَرُ سَيِّداً كُهُولِ أَهْلِ الْجَنَّةِ مِنَ الْأَوَّلِينَ وَ الْآخِرِينَ إِلَّا النَّبِيِّينَ وَ الْمُرْسَلِينَ.

"He (ﷺ) said, The Messenger of Allāh said: 'Abū Bakr and 'Umar are the leaders of the mature people of Paradise, the

first and the last, except for the Prophets and the Messengers."[11]

So based upon this, the most superior of humanity to enter paradise after the Prophets and Messengers are Abū Bakr and ʿUmar (رَضِيَ اللَّهُ عَنْهُ) who are the best of humanity after the Prophets.

A narration mentioned in Ṣaḥīḥ al-Bukhārī on the authority of Ibn ʿUmar (رَضِيَ اللَّهُ عَنْهُمَا) in which he said,

كُنَّا نُخَيِّرُ بَيْنَ النَّاسِ فِي زَمَنِ النَّبِيِّ صَلَّى اللهُ عَلَيْهِ، فَنُخَيِّرُ أَبَا بَكْرٍ، ثُمَّ عُمَرَ بْنَ الْخَطَّابِ، ثُمَّ عُثْمَانَ بْنَ عَفَّانَ رَضِيَ اللهُ عَنْهُمْ وَ فِي زِيَادَةٍ

[11]Collected by Ahmad (602) and at-Tirmidhī (3666), and Ibn Mājah (95) which was reported by a group of the Companions and Shaykh al-Albānī graded it to be Ṣaḥīḥ by various chains in his book Ṣaḥīḥ (824).

عِنْدَ غَيْرِهِ: ((فَيَبْلُغُ ذَلِكَ النَّبِيَّ صَلَّى اللهُ عَلَيْهِ وَسَلَّمَ فَلَا يُنْكِرُهُ)).

"We used to compare the people as to who was better during the lifetime of Allāh's Messenger (ﷺ). We used to regard Abū Bakr as the best, then `Umar, and then ʿUthmān ."[12]

It is mentioned in Ṣaḥīḥ al-Bukhārī on the authority of Muḥammad ibn al-Ḥanafiyyah that he said, **"I said, 'Alī ibn Abū Tālib (رضي الله عنه), which people are the best after the Messenger of Allāh (ﷺ)?' He said, 'Abū Bakr', I then said, 'Then who?' He said, 'Then ʿUmar'; and I was**

[12]Collected by ibn Abū Ā'sim (993) in his book *as-Sunnah;* collected by Abū Ya'lā (5604) in his book *al-Musnad;* collected by at-Ṭabari (1764) in his book Musnad ash-Shāmīyah; Shaykh al-Albānī graded it to be Ṣaḥīḥ in his book *Zalāl al-Jannah* (1193).

afraid that he was going to say ʿUthmān. So I said, 'Then you!' He said, 'I am only one of the Muslims.'" This was Alī (رَضِيَ ٱللَّهُ عَنْهُ).

It is reported by ʿĀli (رَضِيَ ٱللَّهُ عَنْهُ) as what comes in the Book *as-Sunnah* by Ibn Abū A'sim that he said, **"Anyone who would come to me preferring me over Abū Bakr would be flogged as a slanderer."** This was the speech of the leader of the Believers, the rightly-guided successor, Alī ibn Tālib (رَضِيَ ٱللَّهُ عَنْهُ).

Based upon this, it is imperative that we understand and learn from our obligation concerning the Companions and that we are cognizant of the degrees of virtue that are present among them as well as the order and rank of their virtue between them so we can give each one of them their proper due. Didn't Allāh say in the Qur'ān,

﴿ لَا يَسْتَوِي مِنكُم مَّنْ أَنفَقَ مِن قَبْلِ ٱلْفَتْحِ وَقَٰتَلَ ۚ أُو۟لَٰٓئِكَ أَعْظَمُ دَرَجَةً مِّنَ ٱلَّذِينَ أَنفَقُوا۟ مِنۢ بَعْدُ وَقَٰتَلُوا۟ ۚ وَكُلًّا وَعَدَ ٱللَّهُ ٱلْحُسْنَىٰ ۚ وَٱللَّهُ بِمَا تَعْمَلُونَ خَبِيرٌ ﴿١٠﴾ ﴾

"Not equal among you are those who spent and fought before the conquering (of Makkah) (with those among you who did so later). Such are higher in degree than those who spent and fought afterward. But to all, Allāh has promised the best (reward). And Allāh is All-Aware of what you do." [*Sūrah al-Ḥadīd* 57:10]

The word **"al-Ḥusna"** refers to paradise and the word **"al-Fatḥ"** refers to the conquest of Makkah. It has also been said that is intended to mean the treatise of al-Ḥudaybīyyah. So those whose gave a pledge to the Prophet (صَلَّى ٱللَّٰهُ عَلَيْهِ وَسَلَّمَ) under the tree on the day of the treatise of al-Ḥudaybīyyah are not equal in ʾĪmān, status, affair, and degree in comparison with the Companions who accepted Islām after (al-Ḥudaybīyyah) and fought. There is a significant difference between the two; although all of them are Companions, people of ʾĪmān, and are in paradise.

The Companions have degrees of virtue amongst them:

The most virtuous of the Companions are those who made the pledge under the tree, and the most virtuous amongst of them are those who witnessed the battle of Badr, and the most virtuous amongst them all are the ten who have been given the glad tidings of Paradise. These ten from among the Companions of the Prophet (صَلَّى ٱللَّٰهُ عَلَيْهِ وَسَلَّمَ) who attested to that in one sitting that they will enter Paradise. By specifying that they will be in Paradise for eternity (which was mentioned in one sitting), He increased them in dignity and honor. It is mentioned in the Ḥadīth that at-Tirmidhī, Imām Ahmad and others have collected on the authority of ʿAbdur Raḥmān bin Awf (رَضِيَ اللَّهُ عَنْهُ) that he said,

قَالَ : سَمِعْتُ رَسُولَ اللهِ صَلَّى اللهُ عَلَيْهِ وَ سَلَّمَ يَقُولُ : أَبُو بَكْرٍ فِي الْجَنَّةِ ، وَ عُمَرُ فِي الْجَنَّةِ ، وَ عُثْمَانُ فِي الْجَنَّةِ ، وَ عَلِيٌّ فِي الْجَنَّةِ وَ طَلْحَةُ فِي الْجَنَّةِ ، وَ الزُّبَيْرُ فِي الْجَنَّةِ ، وَ عَبْدُ الرَّحْمَنِ ابْنُ عَوْفٍ فِي الْجَنَّةِ ، وَ سَعْدُ بْنُ أَبِي وَقَّاصٍ فِي

الْـجَـنَّـةِ ، وَ سَـعِـيـدُ بْـنُ زَيْـدِ ابْـنِ عَـمْـرِو بْـنِ نُـفَـيْـلٍ فِـي الْـجَـنَّـةِ، وَ أَبُـو عُـبَـيْـدَةَ بْـنُ الْـجَـرَّاحِ فِـي الْـجَـنَّـةِ .

"He said, "that I heard the Messenger of Allāh (ﷺ) said: "Abū Bakr is in Paradise, 'Umar is in Paradise, 'Uthman is in Paradise, 'Alī is in Paradise, Talhah is in Paradise, Az-Zubair is in Paradise, 'Abdur-Rahman bin 'Awf is in Paradise, Sa'd bin Abī Waqqās is in Paradise, Sa'īd is in Paradise, and Abu 'Ubaidah bin Al-Jarrah is in Paradise."[13]

In one sitting, it was attested to by the Prophet (عَلَيْهِ الصَّلَاةُ وَالسَّلَامُ) that these ten individuals will be in

[13]Collected by Ahmad (#1675); at-Tirmidhī (#3747); an-Nasā'ī in the book *al-Kubrā* (#8194) from the Ḥadīth of ʿAbdur Raḥmān bin 'Awf (رَضِيَ اللَّهُ عَنْهُ); and Shaykh al-Albānī declared it to be Ṣaḥīḥ in his book *Ṣaḥīḥ al-Jāmiʿ* (#50).

Paradise. They were on earth knowing that they will be in Paradise. He (عَلَيْهِ ٱلصَّلَاةُ وَٱلسَّلَامُ) the one who is truthful and trustworthy attested to that. How tremendous and honorable is this testimony (because) they, the Companions, were on earth knowing that on the Day of Resurrection they will be amongst the people of Paradise.

The most virtuous of these ten are the four Khulafa (i.e. successors), and the most virtuous of them are Abū Bakr and ʿUmar; and the most virtuous of all the Companions without restriction is Abū Bakr as-Ṣiddīq, the truthful one of the ʾUmmah.

Abū Bakr as-Ṣiddīq (رَضِيَ ٱللَّهُ عَنْهُ) was singled out among all of the Companions due to his companionship (as mentioned) in the Qur'ān,

﴿ إِذْ يَقُولُ لِصَاحِبِهِۦ لَا تَحْزَنْ إِنَّ ٱللَّهَ مَعَنَا ﴾

"And he (صَلَّى ٱللَّهُ عَلَيْهِ وَسَلَّمَ) said to his Companion (Abū Bakr): "Be not sad (or afraid), surely Allāh is with us." [*Sūrah at-Tawbah 9:40*]

There is not a single Companion singled out for their companionship as mentioned in the Qur'ān except Abū Bakr (رَضِيَ ٱللَّهُ عَنْهُ) the truthful one of the ʾUmmah. He is the first of the men to accept Islām. He was truthful; so whatever was related to him of the Prophet (صَلَّى ٱللَّهُ عَلَيْهِ وَسَلَّمَ), he believed in it even when the Prophet came to the Polytheists and informed them that he made a night journey to the "house of al-Maqdas" and then ascended to heaven and rode on the *al-Burāq*. They heard this news, yet they weren't able to believe in it. So they went to Abū Bakr (رَضِيَ ٱللَّهُ عَنْهُ) who said,

إِنْ كَانَ قَالَ ذَلِكَ فَقَدْ صَدَقَ!

"If he said that then it is the truth."[14]

He is the most truthful one of the ʾUmmah (رَضِيَ اللَّهُ عَنْهُ); not a single person will reach his standing in truthfulness. Allāh (سُبْحَانَهُ وَتَعَالَى) says,

﴿ وَالَّذِينَ ءَامَنُوا بِاللَّهِ وَرُسُلِهِ أُولَٰئِكَ هُمُ الصِّدِّيقُونَ ﴾

"And those who believe in (the Oneness of) Allāh and His Messengers, they are the *Siddiqūn*." [*Sūrah al-Hadīd* 57:19]

The first to fall under this honor and surname is Abū Bakr as-Ṣiddīq (رَضِيَ اللَّهُ عَنْهُ) and no one has reached his status in this area.

---

[14] Collected by al-Ḥākim (3/65); and Abū Na'īm in the book *ma'rifah as-Ṣaḥābah* (1/82); and al-Bayhaqī in *Dalaail an-Nubuwah* (2/361) from the Ḥadīth of ʿĀishah. Al-Ḥākim declared it to be Ṣaḥīḥ and adh-Dhahabī agreed. Shaykh al-Albānī also declared it to be Ṣaḥīḥ in his book *as-Ṣaḥīḥah* (306).

Take a look at this profound quality. On one occasion, the Prophet (صَلَّىٱللَّهُعَلَيْهِوَسَلَّمَ) was talking to his Companions and Abū Bakr and ʿUmar were not present. Abū Hurayrah (رَضِيَٱللَّهُعَنْهُ) said,

عَنْ أَبِي هُرَيْرَةَ ـ رضى الله عنه ـ قَالَ صَلَّى رَسُولُ اللَّهِ صلى الله عليه وسلم صَلاَةَ الصُّبْحِ، ثُمَّ أَقْبَلَ عَلَى النَّاسِ، فَقَالَ " بَيْنَا رَجُلٌ يَسُوقُ بَقَرَةً إِذْ رَكِبَهَا فَضَرَبَهَا فَقَالَتْ إِنَّا لَمْ نُخْلَقْ لِهَذَا، إِنَّمَا خُلِقْنَا لِلْحَرْثِ ". فَقَالَ النَّاسُ سُبْحَانَ اللَّهِ بَقَرَةٌ تَكَلَّمُ. فَقَالَ " فَإِنِّي أُومِنُ بِهَذَا أَنَا وَأَبُو بَكْرٍ وَعُمَرُ ـ وَمَا هُمَا ثَمَّ ـ وَبَيْنَمَا رَجُلٌ فِي غَنَمِهِ إِذْ عَدَا الذِّئْبُ فَذَهَبَ مِنْهَا بِشَاةٍ، فَطَلَبَ حَتَّى كَأَنَّهُ اسْتَنْقَذَهَا مِنْهُ، فَقَالَ لَهُ الذِّئْبُ هَذَا اسْتَنْقَذْتَهَا مِنِّي فَمَنْ لَهَا يَوْمَ السَّبُعِ، يَوْمَ لاَ رَاعِيَ لَهَا غَيْرِي ". فَقَالَ النَّاسُ سُبْحَانَ اللَّهِ ذِئْبٌ يَتَكَلَّمُ. قَالَ " فَإِنِّي أُومِنُ بِهَذَا أَنَا وَأَبُو بَكْرٍ وَعُمَرُ ". وَمَا هُمَا ثَمَّ.

"Once Allāh's Messenger (صَلَّى ٱللَّهُ عَلَيْهِ وَسَلَّمَ); offered the morning prayer and then faced the people and said, "While a man was driving a cow, he suddenly rode over to it and beat it. The cow said, "We have not been created for this, but we have been created for sloughing." On that, the people said astonishingly, "Glorified be Allāh! A cow speaks!" The Prophet (صَلَّى ٱللَّهُ عَلَيْهِ وَسَلَّمَ) said, "I believe this, and Abu Bakr and `Umar believe it too, although neither of them was present there. While a person was amongst his sheep, a wolf attacked and took one of the sheep. The man chased the wolf till he saved it from the wolf. After that the wolf said, 'You have saved it from me; but who will guard it on the day of the wild beasts when there will be no shepherd to guard them except me (because of riots and afflictions)? ' The people said surprisingly,

"Glorified be Allāh! A wolf speaks!" The Prophet (صَلَّى ٱللَّهُ عَلَيْهِ وَسَلَّمَ) said, "But I believe this, and Abū Bakr and `Umar too."[15]

Look at Abū as-Ṣiddīq and his ʾĪmān and look at the complete guidance of the Companions (رَضِيَ ٱللَّهُ عَنْهُمْ). If we were to start discussing the virtues of Abū Bakr and ʿUmar (رَضِيَ ٱللَّهُ عَنْهُمَا) specifically through the Qur'ān and Sunnah of the Prophet (صَلَّى ٱللَّهُ عَلَيْهِ وَسَلَّمَ) one lecture or several lectures would not suffice. Neither would a single lesson or several suffice due to the abundant virtues and special qualities that have to do with these two Companions (رَضِيَ ٱللَّهُ عَنْهُمَا).

Based upon this, we should devote ourselves to Allāh (عَزَّ وَجَلَّ) and ask Him by His Most Beautiful Names and Lofty Attributes—that He is Allāh

[15]Collected by al-Bukhārī (#3471).

Who there is no deity worthy of worship except for He—that He doesn't make hatred in our hearts for any of the Companions of the Prophet (صَلَّى ٱللَّهُ عَلَيْهِ وَسَلَّمَ) nor any of the Believers; and that may He forgive us and our brothers who preceded us in ʾĪmān.

We ask Allāh (جَلَّ وَعَلَا) by His Most Beautiful Names and Lofty Attributes that He gather us on the Day of Resurrection in the company of his noble Prophet and Companions.

We ask Allāh (جَلَّ وَعَلَا) that He gather us on the Day of Resurrection in the company of Abū Bakr, ʿUmar, ʿUthmān, Alī, and the wives of our Prophet (صَلَّى ٱللَّهُ عَلَيْهِ وَسَلَّمَ)—May Allāh be pleased with them; and that He gather us on the Day of Resurrection in the company of all of the Companions—those who have high status and stations.

ADVICE: GIVING CONCERN TO STUDYING THE BIOGRAPHIES OF THE COMPANIONS (رَضِيَ اللَّهُ عَنْهُمْ)

It is befitting for us—O brothers in Islām—to give great concern towards studying the circumstances of the Companions and their special qualities, as well as virtues. Starting with what is mentioned in the Noble Qur'ān, then what is mentioned in the Sunnah of the Noble Prophet (عَلَيْهِ الصَّلَاةُ وَالسَّلَامُ).

Then, also, what is mentioned from the blessed statements and tremendous transmissions that the Imāms of Islām and the scholars of the religion authored in the books of Ḥadīth, similarly to what is mentioned in Ṣaḥīḥ al-Bukhārī, Ṣaḥīḥ Muslim, the four books of Sunan, and the books of Musnad; in addition to those specific books which exclusively mention the virtues of the Companions so that we can take benefit from these readings in many ways. From them are:

1st Benefit: That when you read about the Companions and their reports, biographies, and Ḥadīth indeed you will increase in love, praise, making Du'ā for them (رَضِيَ ٱللَّهُ عَنْهُمْ), seeking forgiveness for them, and mentioning them in a good way—this will suffice as a benefit.

2nd Benefit: That you be devoted when reading their biographies in order to model yourself after them. Every time you model yourself after the Companions, you become closer to good; and every time you increase in modeling yourself after the Companions and their path and methodology—clinging to their way, you will become among the closest of people that are upon good; because Allāh (عَزَّوَجَلَّ) says,

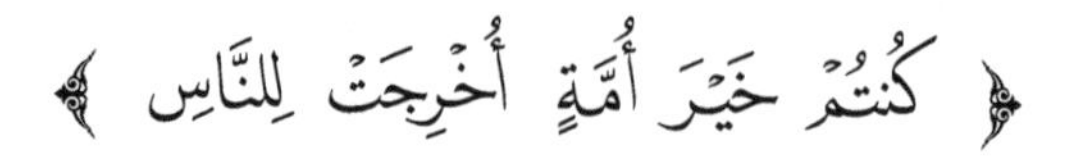

"You are the best of peoples ever raised up for mankind You [true believers in Islāmic Monotheism, and real followers of Prophet Muḥammad (ﷺ) and his *Sunnah* (legal ways, etc.)] are the best of peoples ever raised up for mankind" [*Sūrah 'Alī ʿImrān 3:110*]

And the Prophet (ﷺ) said,

خَـيْـرُ الـنَّـاسِ قَـرْنِـي

"The best of mankind is my generation."[16]

These individuals were attested to by Allāh and His Messenger (ﷺ) as to their excellence and every time you increase in modeling

[16]Collected by al-Bukhārī (#2652, 3651, 6429); Muslim (#2533) from the Ḥadīth of Ibn Mas'ūd (رَضِيَ اللَّهُ عَنْهُ).

yourself after them you will come closer to being upon good.

3rd Benefit: That you become more distant from disparaging them (i.e. the Companions), reviling them or similar to that. You have been ordered to seek forgiveness for them, commend them, laud them and show honor and respect towards the Companions of the Prophet (صَلَّى ٱللَّهُ عَلَيْهِ وَسَلَّمَ). Hence, reading their biographies will increase you in having love for them, praising them and extolling them, as well as making Du'ā that Allāh be pleased with them. It also keeps one distant from speaking ill of them unjustly.

THE CORRECT STANCE OF THE MUSLIM TOWARDS WHAT HAPPENED AMONG THE COMPANIONS (رَضِيَ ٱللَّهُ عَنْهُمْ)

Here is the last matter which is related to what occurred among the Companions: differing. So what are we obliged to do on this occasion concerning what happened among them (رَضِيَ ٱللَّهُ عَنْهُمْ).

We will highlight on this (topic) a statement of one of the Salaf when he was asked about this matter. He said,

تِلْكَ فِتْنَةٌ طَهَّرَ اللهُ مِنْهَا سُيُوفَنَا ، فَلْنُطَهِّرْ مِنْهَا أَلْسِنَتَنَا .

"Allāh cleansed our swords of this fitnah; so we should purify our tongues of it."[17]

Another one of the Salaf was asked also about a similar matter and he recited the statement of Allāh (سُبْحَانَهُۥ وَتَعَالَىٰ),

﴿ تِلْكَ أُمَّةٌ قَدْ خَلَتْ لَهَا مَا كَسَبَتْ وَلَكُم مَّا كَسَبْتُمْ وَلَا تُسْـَٔلُونَ عَمَّا كَانُوا۟ يَعْمَلُونَ ﴿١٣٤﴾ ﴾

"That was a nation who has passed away. They shall receive the reward of what they earned and you of what you earn. And you will not be asked of what they used to do." [*Sūrah al-Baqarah* 2:134]

---

[17] Reported from 'Umar bin 'Abdul Azīz (رَحِمَهُ ٱللَّهُ); look in the book *Hilyah al-Awliyā* (9/114) and in the book *al-Mujālisah* (#1965) with the wording, **"Allāh cleansed my hands of this blood so why should I tinge my tongue concerning it?!"**

So let's presume that one of the Companions made a mistake—will Allāh (عَزَّوَجَلَّ) hold you accountable on the day of Resurrection for that mistake? Allāh (سُبْحَانَهُوَتَعَالَىٰ) says,

﴿ وَلَا تُسْـَٔلُونَ عَمَّا كَانُوا۟ يَعْمَلُونَ ١٣٤ ﴾

"And you will not be asked of what they used to do." [*Sūrah al-Baqarah 2:134*]

So why would you involve yourself with that which happened among the Companions when you are not a reckoner or observer over them. Allāh says,

﴿ تِلْكَ أُمَّةٌ قَدْ خَلَتْ ۖ لَهَا مَا كَسَبَتْ وَلَكُم مَّا كَسَبْتُمْ ۖ وَلَا تُسْـَٔلُونَ عَمَّا كَانُوا۟ يَعْمَلُونَ ١٣٤ ﴾

"That was a nation who has passed away. They shall receive the reward of what they earned and you of what you earn. And you will not be asked of what they used to do." [*Sūrah al-Baqarah* 2:134]

Another matter which is of the utmost importance. This mistake which presume came about from some the Companions; so we have

to judge this matter according to what Islām says. The Prophet (عَلَيْهِ ٱلصَّلَاةُ وَٱلسَّلَامُ) said,

إِذَا حَكَمَ الْحَاكِمُ فَاجْتَهَدَ ثُمَّ أَصَابَ فَلَهُ أَجْرَانِ ،

وَ إِذَا حَكَمَ فَاجْتَهَدَ ثُمَّ أَخْطَأَ فَلَهُ أَجْرٌ .

"When a judge gives a ruling, having tried his best to decide correctly, and is right (in his decision), he will have a double reward; and when he gives a ruling having tried his

best to decide correctly, and is wrong (in his decision), he will have a single reward. "[18]

So based upon this, matters which have been reported by the Companions related to differing or mistakes are of two circumstances:

❖ Either it is a lie against them, and this is most of what has been reported/relayed.

❖ Or either it is correct and affirmed; and whatever has been authenticated from them concerning that (matter) then they (i.e., Companions) are Mujtahidūn in the matter. So, either one of them is a Mujtahid who is correct and he receives two rewards, or either he is a Mujtahid who erred and he

[18]Collected by al-Bukhārī (#7352) and Muslim (#1716) from the Ḥadīth of ʿUmar bin al-'Ās (رَضِيَ اللَّهُ عَنْهُ).

receives one reward and his mistake/sin is forgiven.

Hence, it is inappropriate for one at this point to plunge into something that occurred among the Companions unless one wanted to protect and defend their honor; clarifying their status, worth, and their affair (رَضِيَ ٱللَّهُ عَنْهُمْ).

I will be concluding this treatise with this supplication. I say,

"O Allāh! Send Ṣalāh upon Muḥammad and the family of Muḥammad just as You sent Ṣalāh upon ʾIbrāhīm and the family of ʾIbrāhīm; indeed, You are All-Praiseworthy and Exalted. O Allāh! Bless Muḥammad and the family of Muḥammad just as You have blessed ʾIbrāhīm and the family of ʾ Ibrāhīm, indeed You Are All-Praiseworthy and Exalted."

"O Allāh! Be pleased with the rightly-guided successors and Imams, Abū Bakr as-Ṣiddīq, ʿUmar al-Farūq, ʿUthmān Dhul-Nurayn, and Alī ibn Abū Tālib. O Allāh! Be pleased with the remaining ten Companions who were given glad tidings of Paradise. O Allāh! Be pleased with the wives of your Prophet (صَلَّىٱللَّهُعَلَيْهِوَسَلَّمَ). O Allāh! Be pleased with the Companions of your Prophet who were present at Badr and at the pledge of Ridwan. O Allāh! Be pleased with all of the Companions of your Prophet and those who followed them in best.

O Our Lord! Forgive us and our brothers who have preceded us in ʾĪmān, and please don't make within our hearts rancor for those who have believed. O Our Lord! Indeed, you are Most Benevolent, Most Merciful.

O Allāh! We ask you to free us and we seek refuge with you, O Possessor of Majesty and Honor, from the path of those who revile anyone of the Companions of the Prophet (صَلَّى ٱللَّهُ عَلَيْهِ وَسَلَّمَ). O Allāh! We ask you to free us from those individuals and we seek refuge with You, O Possessor of Majesty and Honor, from their way."

"We ask You, O Possessor of Majesty and Honor, to fill our hearts with love for all of the Companions of Your Prophet and that You gather us in their company on the Day of Resurrection, O Possessor of Majesty and Honor."

"O Allāh! Forgive us all. O Allāh! Grant us Tawfīq in what You love and are pleased with and aid us upon righteous and piety."

"O Allāh! We ask you for what necessitates your mercy and forgiveness, the spoils of every good deed, safety from every sin, success to enter Paradise and safety from entering Hell."

"O Allāh! Rectify for us our religion which is a defense for our affairs. Rectify for us our worldly life which we live in. Rectify for us our Hereafter which is our final abode. Make our life as an increase for everything that is good and make our death an ease for us from every evil."

"O Allāh! Rectify matters among us and join our hearts. Guide us to the paths to peace. Take us out of the darkness and into the light. Bless us in our hearing, sight, and strength as long as You give us life."

"O Allāh! Gather us upon obedience to You, O Possessor of Majesty and Honor, and gather us upon whatever brings us close to You and causes our scales to be heavy, O the Ever Living, the One

Who sustains and protects all that exists! O Possessor of Majesty and Honor!"

"O Allāh! Make us among those who hear the Statement and follow it in the best manner. These individuals whom Allāh has guided, they are the people of intellect."

Our last call is that all Praise belongs to Allāh, the Lord of all that exists. May Allāh raise his rank and bless his mention; May Allāh bestow blessings upon His servant and Messenger, our Prophet Muḥammad, his family and all of his Companions.

Made in the USA
Columbia, SC
10 October 2022

69151680R00059